Woman Warrior for Christ

90-Day Devotional

Encouraging Women to Fight the Good Fight of Faith

by

Sister Soldiers in Christ

The Three Sisters Publishing
San Angelo, Texas

Three Sisters Publishing
800 W. Ave. D., #2NE
San Angelo, Texas 76903

Author's Note: This is a work of nonfiction. There is no intention by the author to write about a specific situation effecting known or unknown persons, nor is there any natural knowledge, of specific situations and circumstances encountered by actual people, living or dead, or businesses, events, institutions, or locales. It is the author's contention that this work is a work inspired by the Father, Son, and Holy Spirit and may directly, without the knowledge of the author, speak to individual situations and circumstances.

Book Layout ©2017 BookDesignTemplates.com

Ordering Information:
Book can be purchased online or through SisterSoldiersinChrist.com For special rates on quantity sales, contact the address above or email: info@SisterSoldiersInChrist.com.

Woman Warrior for Christ 90-Day Devotional / Sister Soldiers in Christ -- 1st ed.

Italics added to Scripture quotations or other font variations are the author's own emphasis.

ISBN 978-1—546998952

To David—the love of my life.

To Sister Bobbye—a true woman warrior.

Most of All—To Jesus Christ, our Lord and Savior.

Fight the good fight of faith,
lay hold on eternal life, to which you were also called
and have confessed the good confession
in the presence of many witnesses.

(1 Timothy 6:12)

Introduction

Who is the woman warrior for Christ? She is the elementary school teacher, coffee shop barista, night-shift nurse, bank president, grocery store clerk, stay-at-home mom, construction engineer, and pastor's wife. She is single, married, widowed, and divorced. She is every shade, shape, and age.

Though intrinsically unique, every woman warrior is fiercely devoted to the Lord. She will not cower at the plans and attacks of the enemy, but perseveres in the face of obstacles. She knows she is never alone.

The woman warrior for Christ is armed with the word of God and dangerous to the kingdom of darkness. Her power and might only come through the Lord of Angel Armies, and when she prays, He shows up.

She knows what it is like to get knocked down, but she also knows what it is like to get back up. She believes that victory is imminent and remains steadfast in the faith. Ultimately, the woman warrior for Christ is that woman who bows her heart at the word and will of her Lord.

She is faithful. She is valiant. She is HIS.

Four simple steps to use your devotional...

We know that time is precious and want you to get the most you can from these daily devotionals. Following are *four easy steps* to make that happen:

- Pray before you read every devotional, asking the Holy Spirit to reveal what He would have you specifically see and hear. It is the Father's desire to commune with you. Let these pages speak life to your spirit.

- Choose the time of day to read your daily devotional that is best for you, when distractions are limited and Jesus has your focus. Remember, it is not a chore, but a time of sweet fellowship between you and your Lord.

- After you read, ask the Holy Spirit what He desires to say to you. Write what you believe He is speaking on the *From His Heart to Mine* page that adjoins every daily devotional. You don't have to get it perfect. It may be one word, one sentence, or one paragraph. Just write.

- Close your devotional time with prayer. Remember to make mention of all your Sister Soldiers in Christ who are also sharing in the pages of their own daily devotional. Know that you will be in our prayers as well. God bless you on your 90-day journey.

An Intimate Love

The woman warrior has but one desire for the days ahead: To Know Him MORE. No more masks of pretense to impress others or pacify her ego. She is DONE with fake.

She wants to get real with God. While the world offers placebo religion, seeking to keep her spiritually sedated and ineffectual, she knows He is not in those places. She knows that the ABUNDANT LIFE resides in knowing HIM—intimately and personally.

Promises unravel, resolutions break, and commitments fall apart, but HER LORD will not disappoint! She sets her hope in KNOWING Him.

And when He had removed him, He raised up for them David as king, to whom also He gave testimony and said, 'I have found David the son of Jesse, a man after My own heart, who will do all My will.' (Acts 13:22)

From His Heart to Mine . . .

DAY 2
Childlike Faith

Inside of EVERY woman warrior is a FEARLESS child. She laughs at adversity and leaps over obstacles without thought of harm. Her feet follow in the footsteps of her FATHER, knowing that He is leading her along a sovereign path and looking over His shoulder to be sure she follows.

Because she knows her position as a daughter of the King, CONFIDENCE is her crown. When the rain comes, she jumps into the water puddles without thought of drowning. Life's trials do not hinder her or hold her back! She knows what it is like to slip and fall, but she also knows that the Lord's hand will lift her back up.

He has never left her in the mud or mire. He washes her clean and sets her back on her feet to leap another day.

Her Father finds delight in her, and she delights in Him!

Show Your marvelous lovingkindness by Your right hand, O You who save those who trust in You From those who rise up against them. (Psalm 17:7)

From His Heart to Mine . . .

Overflowing Joy

The woman warrior protects her JOY for in it is her STRENGTH. She knows it is a bullseye for the enemy. Satan recognizes the threat, and seeks to destroy it.

When JOY flows, POWER flows—

Power to break chains, power to destroy prison walls, and power to set the captives free. True joy is not a fake smile or pretend laughter, but a DIVINE inner knowing that JESUS REIGNS!

No demon in hell, or darkness of night, can contain a woman warrior wielding the power of JOY. Lord God, we need MORE JOY!

But at midnight Paul and Silas were praying and singing hymns to God, and the prisoners were listening to them. Suddenly there was a great earthquake, so that the foundations of the prison were shaken; and immediately all the doors were opened and everyone's chains were loosed. (Acts 16:25-26)

From His Heart to Mine . . .

Strong Finisher

She is not a woman warrior because her life is pristine and perfect. Not even close! She is a warrior woman for Christ BECAUSE she presses on toward the HIGH CALL despite what life throws at her.

Others may retreat or surrender, but "give-up" is not in her present or her future. She is a force to be reckoned with, because of two reasons: she draws her strength from the Lord AND keeps her eyes on the prize!

When she stumbles or falls, she gets back up and goes at it again. She will stay the course; she will finish the battle! She will win the war! She IS a WARRIOR for CHRIST.

Brethren, I do not count myself to have apprehended; but one thing I do, forgetting those things which are behind and reaching forward to those things which are ahead. I press toward the goal for the prize of the upward call of God in Christ Jesus. (Philippians 3:13-14)

From His Heart to Mine . . .

Thought Leader

The woman warrior for Christ knows that her greatest battles begin in her mind. "Go this way." "No! Go that way." "Do this." "No! Do that." The Lord is not the author of confusion! When she walks in His PRESENCE and His PEACE, there is a calmness to her thoughts and a quiet confidence.

She will not let fear, self-protection, vain ambition, past failure or even the plots and plans of others dictate her decisions. Ultimately, her allegiance and obedience belong to Christ Jesus. While her flesh may squirm and scream to have its way, the woman warrior takes her thoughts captive—not the other way around!

She surrenders her mind to the WORD and WILL of her Lord. No one else will protect her like Him. No one else will guide her like Him. And no one, absolutely NO ONE, will ever love her like Him.

For where envy and self-seeking exist, confusion and every evil thing are there. But the wisdom that is from above is first pure, then peaceable, gentle, willing to yield, full of mercy and good fruits, without partiality and without hypocrisy. (James 3:16-17)

From His Heart to Mine . . .

Guarding Her Sword

You will not find her sword hanging on her living room wall as an impotent decoration to be admired but never touched. You will not find her sword rolling around in the backseat floorboard of her car along with a pair of flip-flops and an empty water bottle. You will not find her sword under her bed, dusty and forgotten, along with all her scrapbook memorabilia.

YOU WILL find her sword at her side, within her heart, and on her lips—ready to use at a second's notice! The woman warrior for Christ knows she is armed and dangerous because she carries the Word of God, the SWORD OF THE SPIRIT, wherever she goes. Power is alive in her through HIS WORD. Speak it! Believe it!

For the word of God is living and powerful, and sharper than any two-edged sword, piercing even to the division of soul and spirit ... (Hebrews 4:12)

From His Heart to Mine . . .

DAY 7

A Joyful Spirit

LAUGH OFTEN! The woman warrior is not so somber and serious that she has no room in her day for pleasure. Experience has taught her that laughter in the time of trials confuses and confounds the enemy. Laughter spiritually alters her surroundings and births beauty where the enemy expects to see ashes of bitterness.

Laughter is also an expression of her faith, proof that she APPRECIATES the life God has given her and intends to FULLY ENJOY her brief sojourn upon earth. She knows the time is near when she will no longer walk by faith but will see HIM as He is—in all His glory. For now, she chooses to HONOR HIM by enjoying the life He gave her.

To console those who mourn in Zion, To give them beauty for ashes, The oil of joy for mourning, The garment of praise for the spirit of heaviness; That they may be called trees of righteousness, The planting of the Lord, that He may be glorified. (Isaiah 61:3)

From His Heart to Mine . . .

Never the Same

She met a MAN. She just "happened" to be at the well when He walked up. He looked her in the eye—something unheard of in her day! He looked deeper, all the way into her soul.

He looked at her like no man ever had. He looked at her like He truly valued her, as a priceless, irreplaceable jewel. The best part—He knew everything she wanted to hide in her life, and yet, there was NO condemnation. Only compassion. Only love.

From that moment forward, she knew she would NEVER be the same. The Messiah changed her life. How can she help but worship Him? How can she help but tell others about Him!

The woman said to Him, "I know that Messiah is coming" (who is called Christ). "When He comes, He will tell us all things." Jesus said to her, "I who speak to you am He. (John 4:25-26)

From His Heart to Mine . . .

An Open Door

The woman warrior knows there is POWER in the BLOOD of Jesus. She does not take it lightly; it is not to be trampled on or treated as ordinary. The blood that closed the door on the enemy's reign opened the door to the throne room of God.

She now has a relationship with the very Creator. She doesn't have to wait to hear the Prophet speak. Her Lord knows her voice and gives her audience!

She will spend the day being grateful to the ONE who made it possible, the ONE who loved her without limits, and the ONE who said she was worth it all. She will not ask for anything today. She will simply be THANKFUL for the precious blood of JESUS CHRIST— the blood shed for the world. The blood shed for *her*.

...To Him who loved us and washed us from our sins in His own blood, and has made us kings and priests to His God and Father, to Him be glory and dominion forever and ever. Amen. (Revelation 1:5-6)

From His Heart to Mine . . .

Melt the Chains

There is FREEDOM in the FIRE. It is hot in the flames. No denying that fact! Even still, the woman warrior does not have to let the trials and tribulations of life keep her bound. She knows the Lord is with her, no matter how hot the pit.

Experience has taught her not to resist the heat. It is the fire that often burns away what binds her. Whether it is anger, unforgiveness, addiction, sexual sin, insecurity, jealousy, or fear—she will trust the LORD!

There is no fear in the fire! Her Lord shields her! He does not let the fire consume her! He uses the flames to free her.

Then King Nebuchadnezzar was astonished; and he rose in haste and spoke, saying to his counselors, "Did we not cast three men bound into the midst of the fire?" They answered and said to the king, "True, O king." "Look!" he answered, "I see four men loose, walking in the midst of the fire; and they are not hurt, and the form of the fourth is like the Son of God." (Daniel 3:24-26)

From His Heart to Mine . . .

The Lion Roars

The enemy made a mistake. He overestimated his influence AND underestimated her resolve. Did he think her that easy of a target? Big mistake! Her voice may be gentle and her touch tender, but in her chest beats the fire and fierceness of a warrior's heart!

When he came after those she loves, he crossed the line. Not because of her strength and might—she knows she is but dust. But because of her faith in JESUS. The very One who crushed the head of the serpent, defeated death, and claimed eternal victory LIVES on the inside of her.

HE is NOT afraid. He will not surrender. He will rebuke Satan! Nothing or no one can overcome HIM. He is the LION from the tribe of JUDAH. The victory is already sealed. Satan—step back!

A thousand may fall at your side, And ten thousand at your right hand; But it shall not come near you. Only with your eyes shall you look, And see the reward of the wicked. (Psalm 91:7-8)

From His Heart to Mine . . .

DAY 12

Beautiful Cross

Jesus said to carry "your" cross. The woman warrior knows that she does not have the grace to carry a cross that belongs to another. The cross she carries is hers alone.

She also knows that the cares of this world grow dim under the shadow of her cross. When her mind, will, and emotions demand their way, she remembers what is in her hands. The beautiful wooden cross, stained with her tears, is proof of her sacrifice. It is evidence of daily death to her loud flesh, vain ambitions, and self-centered will.

When the trials come, and Satan urges her to let go, she will cling even more tightly—knowing that her Lord will not let her stumble or fall. She is not a feeble soldier in the Lord's army. She WILL carry her cross. The rest is in His hands.

...being confident of this very thing, that He who has begun a good work in you will complete it until the day of Jesus Christ ... (Philippians 1:6)

From His Heart to Mine . . .

Through God's Eyes

The woman warrior for Christ left "perfection" behind a long time ago. Her heart does not seek praise, but beauty on the inside where there is the greatest return on investment. Outward beauty fades. God sees the heart!

Of course, she cares about how she looks; she is just not obsessed with it or a victim of the latest trend. Vanity is not an idol in her life! She wants to be healthy and whole but will not chase mirrors or the admiration of a man's eye.

Others can judge her for her less than magazine-perfect looks. She is a woman with a HEART AFTER GOD, and there is nothing more beautiful in His sight.

Do not let your adornment be merely outward—arranging the hair, wearing gold, or putting on fine apparel—rather let it be the hidden person of the heart, with the incorruptible beauty of a gentle and quiet spirit, which is very precious in the sight of God. (1 Peter 3:3-4)

From His Heart to Mine . . .

Faithful Follower

SILENCE. Today, the woman warrior did not hear her Lord's voice. She prayed and she listened, but every turn of her head was only met with silence. It was a day when she really NEEDED to hear from Him. So, what now?

The woman warrior does not stop moving. She will not desert her position. She keeps walking, following the last order her Commander gave AND trusting that He is still in charge of the ranks.

This is a time of testing, when she simply puts one foot in front of the other. This is a WALK of FAITH and He is FAITHFUL. She will be the same!

For we walk by faith, not by sight. (2 Corinthians 5:7)

From His Heart to Mine . . .

No More Walls

The day came when the LORD spoke: "Take down your walls."
He had work for the woman warrior to do—battles to fight and souls
to set free. The work could not be done while locked inside the prison
of offense or the shackles of self-protection. She had wasted enough
time in those places!

"But, Lord, this is my safe place!"

He reminded her that HE ALONE is the cleft in the rock, the
shelter in the storm, and the strong tower the enemy cannot conquer.
She is not her own savior. It is time to take down the walls, once and
for all. It is time to focus outward instead of inward. The Spirit of the
Lord is upon her. It is time to change lives. Thank you, Jesus!

*The Spirit of the Lord is upon Me, Because He has anointed Me To preach the
gospel to the poor; He has sent Me to heal the brokenhearted, To proclaim liberty
to the captives And recovery of sight to the blind, To set at liberty those who are
oppressed; To proclaim the acceptable year of the Lord. (Luke 4:18-19)*

From His Heart to Mine . . .

DAY 16
Living Water

"Drink from MY well." She heard the words so clearly. "What well, Lord?"

Too many times, people are willing to drink what the world offers: criticism, lust, discouragement, poverty, pornography, frustration, rage, lewdness, and defeat. But the well of the Lord holds ONLY Living Water—those that drink from His well will never thirst again.

Those who drink from HIM will receive of Him—Peace, Righteousness, Holiness, Encouragement, Hope, and Salvation. Why would anyone want to drink from the world's corrupted cistern when they can submerge themselves in pure, living water?

The woman warrior THINKS before she takes in anything. Only that which is lovely and pure will touch her lips.

Finally, brethren, whatever things are true, whatever things are noble, whatever things are just, whatever things are pure, whatever things are lovely, whatever things are of good report, if there is any virtue and if there is anything praiseworthy—meditate on these things. (Philippians 4:8)

From His Heart to Mine . . .

Her Birthright

The woman warrior does not have to plead or beg to be heard by the King. She walks into His chambers with boldness, bowing her knee and her heart before the One who has bestowed His great love upon her. It is a privilege to belong in His courts—an honor to stand in His presence!

While the enemy will whisper that she has no right and does not belong, the Holy Spirit reminds her that she is sealed with a promise. She is a joint-heir with Christ Jesus. She is precious and valued in the eye of the very One who formed her in her mother's womb and who gave His life for her own.

No longer will she doubt His goodness toward her. She is royalty and crowned with FAVOR. Her Father is the King! There is no fear or shame in his presence. Because of His great love . . . Favor is her birthright!

I in them, and You in Me; that they may be made perfect in one, and that the world may know that You have sent Me, and have loved them as you have loved Me. (John 17:23)

From His Heart to Mine . . .

Choosing Humility

The woman warrior knows her strength is not in herself. Just when she starts thinking she's "all that" then the ground shifts beneath her feet, and she remembers that she is but dust.

It is her LORD who gives her strength; her LORD who sustains her. When self-sufficiency and pride cry out, demanding to be seen or to act, she reminds herself of who she is and who HE is in her.

She praises HIM for what He has brought her TO and THROUGH! She will not interfere this time—creating an Ishmael where God wants to give her an Isaac. She will wait on HIM. She will depend on HIM.

What is man that You are mindful of him, And the son of man that You visit him? For You have made him a little lower than the angels, And You have crowned him with glory and honor. (Psalm 8:4-5)

From His Heart to Mine . . .

Fear No Evil

Why is she surprised trouble surrounds her? When light clashes
with dark, there is always a battle. The woman warrior knows she is a
target; that is why she wears her armor every day. She also knows that
light overcomes darkness. Her God is greater than any minion from
the enemy's camp.

She will pray for the lost souls, especially those who seek to
destroy her reputation and create havoc in her life. Those are the ones
who need Him the most! At the same time, she will not put herself in
harm's way. She will pray for discernment. She will follow the leading
of the Holy Spirit. She will trust the Prince of Peace.

*These things I have spoken to you, that in Me you may have peace. In the world
you will have tribulation; but be of good cheer, I have overcome the world. (John
16:33)*

From His Heart to Mine . . .

DAY 20
Others Minded

Life is hectic. The woman warrior for Christ reminds herself to refocus and choose to be others minded. In the rush of daily life, she often forgets there are people all around her who are struggling, hurting, and in despair.

The clerk scanning her groceries just lost her daughter to cancer. The man who changed her tire on the side of the road needs a job. The older woman at the school crosswalk is estranged from her children, and has shed more tears than she can count.

Oh, how easy it is to walk right past people in need, feeling content with her own life. How easy it is to get caught up in her daily "to-do" list and forget that souls are what matter most. She will purpose this day to focus on others—offering a word in due season, a smile, a compliment, or even a gift. Whatever she can do today, she will do.

But a certain Samaritan, as he journeyed, came where he was. And when he saw him, he had compassion. (Luke 10:33)

From His Heart to Mine . . .

Holding Her Stance

And so it ended. SUDDENLY. How did that happen and why didn't she see it coming? Lord, where was my warning? This was something I NEEDED to know.

If she had only been aware, her sword would have been drawn and ready. But this slithered up to her and hit her between the eyes—knocking her sideways before she realized what happened.

The woman warrior will not stay dazed for long. She WILL rise, and fight even fiercer than before. What the enemy thinks was a fatal blow was only his undoing—not hers!

The lesson? She will not let her guard down, for the enemy is always looking for an opportune time—when she is distracted, busy, weary, or simply forgetful of the battle surrounding her. Thank you, Lord, for reminding me to be vigilant of the enemy and his tactics. I will not make that mistake again!

Be sober, be vigilant; because your adversary the devil walks about like a roaring lion, seeking whom he may devour. (1 Peter 5:8)

From His Heart to Mine . . .

Courage to Confront

Courage is a prized commodity in the woman warrior's arsenal. She calls upon her LORD to take away the fear, insecurity, and reluctance that hinder her from confronting what needs to be confronted. Oh, how much more peaceful her life would be if she did not have to address controlling people and their behaviors. But this has gone on long enough. A manipulative spirit will not determine her destiny!

While others may not like her decisions and even throw angry darts her way, she will not be drawn into the fray. She knows that is just another form of manipulation and will not return evil for evil. Her LORD will shield her as she purposes to walk in love—keeping her conscience clean, her words kind, and her eyes on JESUS.

The LORD is her Commander and the Holy Spirit her Guide— she will not surrender that role to another. Thank you, Jesus for the COURAGE to CONFRONT.

Then Saul said to Samuel, "I have sinned, for I have transgressed the commandment of the Lord and your words, because I feared the people and obeyed their voice. (1 Samuel 15:24)

From His Heart to Mine . . .

Fruit of the Spirit

She doesn't have the same roommates. Shame, regret, depression. They once lived with her, along with a few of their friends—guilt, despair, and self-pity. But the day she met JESUS and welcomed Him inside her heart, her old friends moved out. They were no longer comfortable living in her house. It was swept clean.

NOW, she has new residents sharing her space. By the power and might of the Holy Spirit, she put out the welcome mat for love, joy, peace, longsuffering, kindness, goodness, faithfulness, gentleness, and self-control.

Help us, Lord, to remember the creation you made us in Christ Jesus! We are filled with the fruit of the Spirit.

But the fruit of the Spirit is love, joy, peace, longsuffering, kindness, goodness, faithfulness, gentleness, self-control. Against such there is no law. (Galatians 5:22-23)

From His Heart to Mine . . .

DAY 24
Calm in Confusion

Confusion clutters her mind like a messy closet. She can't find what she is looking for; there are too many distractions in the way. She wants to hear from God, but where is He? In her frantic search, she just makes a messy situation messier.

The woman warrior has learned there are times when she simply must stop, take a deep breath, then go at it much slower. There is no rush. God is not frantic. He is never in a hurry or running late.

Her prayer is that a time comes when she no longer must remind herself to slow down and hear the voice of the Lord. It will be as natural as breathing. But for now . . .

She will trust Him. He is in the calm—not in the chaos.

But those who wait on the Lord
Shall renew their strength;
They shall mount up with wings like eagles,
They shall run and not be weary,
They shall walk and not faint.
(Isaiah 40:31)

From His Heart to Mine . . .

Pride Be Gone

A woman warrior never loses sight of where her strength comes from! She knows too well what happens when she allows self-sufficiency and self-righteousness to rule and reign.

She is not the One who spoke the world into existence. She is not the One who caused the sun and moon to rise and recline in the sky. She is not the One who told the tide where to stop and the winds where to blow. The LORD is not obligated to perform for her!

It is in those times, when pride creeps in and self-will attempts to take over, that she must stop, regroup and submit herself to God's leading once more. Her hope, her prayer, is that one day, she will walk in complete submission to the Spirit. That is where miracles manifest. That is where she seeks to abide.

Until then, Father God, help us! Teach us to walk after the Spirit—not after the flesh. In Jesus' Name.

...'Not by might nor by power, but by My Spirit,' Says the Lord of hosts. (Zechariah 4:6)

From His Heart to Mine . . .

Royal Garments

Though a warrior in the spirit realm, she is much more. She is also ROYALTY—a DAUGHTER of the KING. Truly, what is there for her to fear? She bows her knee to nothing of this world. She only has ONE Lord. Her heart and her hope rest in HIM!

There was a time when she did not know the power and beauty of the promises of her Father. Those days are gone. Now, she walks in the full authority that comes from one who KNOWS her Father is LORD over ALL.

She is covered by HIM and His Word. There is no fear in His perfect love!

She is clothed with strength and dignity; she can laugh at the days to come.
(Proverbs 31:25 / NIV)

From His Heart to Mine . . .

Knowing the Times

The woman warrior knows there is a time to run and a time to REST. She trusts there is a purpose to every season—EVEN the season of delay. Though well-meaning friends may press her to move or to act, she will not be goaded into doing what others would have her do. She recognizes such tactics for what they are and will not be baited.

Though temptation beckons and urgency cries out for her to act, she knows where that noise comes from. If the enemy of her soul cannot get her to walk away from God, he will try to get her to run ahead of Him.

Her deepest desire is to walk in step with God and His will. Nothing will move her from His side. She waits confidently on His PERFECT TIMING.

See then that you walk circumspectly, not as fools but as wise, redeeming the time, because the days are evil. Therefore do not be unwise, but understand what the will of the Lord is. (Ephesians 5:15-17)

From His Heart to Mine . . .

Power of the Sword

The woman warrior's sword is ever SHARP and at the READY.

It is not a weapon she takes for granted. By the grace of God and Him alone, it is part of her very person—a permanent defense that she draws upon to defeat the devil. She knows that the enemy never sets his weapons aside, and neither will she! He is the Father of Lies and they fall continually from his lips.

She is ready to swing the blade of truth and destroy the lies of the enemy at any given time. She knows the Word and the Word lives in her. She also knows it is not her strength, but HIS power and HIS might that will cause the enemy to flee and victory to be established. Praise God for the Sword of the Spirit!

For the word of the Lord is right, And all His work is done in truth. He loves righteousness and justice; The earth is full of the goodness of the Lord. (Psalm 33:4-5)

From His Heart to Mine . . .

DAY 29

Trusting Her Savior

The woman warrior knows that emotions and feelings can be deceptive but the Word of God remains steady and true. When tempted to feel anything contrary to the character of God, she looks to JESUS as her example. He lived in the flesh yet walked out His life on this earth WITHOUT sin.

When feelings and emotions scream in her ear, and the woman warrior knows sin is but a whisper away, she does not pretend everything is perfect. How does that help?! She cries out to the LORD for strength, grace and more grace!

She cannot trust her heart to direct her in time of turmoil. She can only trust her LORD and SAVIOR. "Help me, Jesus, get through this trial without sinning. Help me to see the truth IN ME. Help me to walk more like YOU. In Jesus' Name I pray. Amen."

The heart is deceitful above all things, And desperately wicked; Who can know it? I, the Lord, search the heart, I test the mind, Even to give every man according to his ways, According to the fruit of his doings. (Jeremiah 17:9-10)

From His Heart to Mine . . .

Throne-Room Wisdom

When the woman warrior speaks, wisdom flows through her lips. Her heart's desire is to heal, edify, and instruct—not to bring hurt or harm. She knows that it is ONLY when the divine nature of God speaks through her that true power is present.

It is the Holy Spirit who gives the right words in the right season. It is the Holy Spirit who whispers "silence" when no words are needed. And, it is the Holy Spirit who speaks resurrection life into hopeless, dead situations.

"Father God, please help us to release control of our words to your Holy Spirit so that throne-room wisdom changes hearts and transforms lives. In JESUS' Name."

So teach us to number our days, That we may gain a heart of wisdom. (Psalm 90:12)

From His Heart to Mine . . .

Walking in Freedom

No more chains! The woman warrior knows she is no longer a prisoner of the past. GONE are the days when she wore shackles and heaviness as comfortably as she wore jeans and sandals. She sees herself differently now.

Her eyes opened the moment she welcomed JESUS into her heart, and she is not going back to life in the dungeon. Now, she uses her freedom to show others THE WAY to the abundant life. Fears, addictions, and lies from the enemy cannot stand against a mighty God who has declared her FREE.

Satan has no more right to torment her soul! The very power that raised Christ from the dead lives on the inside of her. Nothing can stand against THAT power! By faith, she believes, receives and walks in FREEDOM.

Therefore if the Son makes you free, you shall be free indeed. (John 8:36)

From His Heart to Mine . . .

Laugh and Let Go

Laughter is her medicine. When she is trying to get out the door, can't find her keys, trips over the dog, finally finds her keys, then loses her cell phone . . . she refuses to get ambushed by annoyance. Life is too short and eternity too long to get caught up in the frustrations of daily living.

She chooses to laugh—at circumstances AND at herself. The One who made heaven and earth is her God. The One who formed man and breathed life into his lungs is her Savior. The One who arranged the planets and orchestrated the orbits is her Father. Why would she worry about little things? She will ENJOY the day.

Little annoyances will not destroy her joy or derail her day. She will choose to rejoice in the Lord. She will say, "Today, I choose to laugh!"

A merry heart does good, like medicine, But a broken spirit dries the bones.
(Proverbs 17:22)

From His Heart to Mine . . .

The Way

There is only ONE WAY to heaven. If the woman warrior listens to those who claim to be wise or enlightened, confusion will call her name like a sea siren calls a sailor.

She refuses to be lured away, captured by the enemy's camp. Her heart, her faith, and her very spirit follow the one and only true God.

Jesus left no doubt. He is the only way. Every other way is a trap—a silken noose that feels good going on, but strangles eternal life for all who dare to wear it. Let your heart not be deceived!

The woman warrior will not let those she loves fall into Satan's clutches without warning. The enemy is out to blind but the HOLY SPIRIT opens eyes to truth. "Father, God, remove the scales from their eyes. Let them see YOU."

Jesus said to him, "I am the way, the truth, and the life. No one comes to the Father except through Me. (John 14:6)

From His Heart to Mine . . .

DAY 34
Occupy the Land

The war ended when Jesus surrendered himself to the cross—the sinless sacrifice—the PERFECT Lamb of God. He now sits victorious at the right hand of the Father. STILL, the battles continue.

The woman warrior pushes back against the enemy, reminding him that he is a defeated foe and has no right to take her loved ones captive. She fights for the territory that already belongs to her—just as the Hebrew children had to take the land that was already their inheritance. So she will TAKE, and KEEP, the new ground.

There will come a time when she can rest. For now, there is work to do. She will not be found lacking. She will continue the good fight, occupying the territory, until her Lord's return.

And he called his ten servants, and delivered them ten pounds, and said unto them, Occupy till I come. (Luke 19:13)

From His Heart to Mine . . .

Better to Sacrifice

The woman warrior recognizes the voice of her Commander. It is the same voice that spoke the world into existence, silenced the shrieks of demons, and called her spirit into newness of life.

He speaks her name with audacious love—a love that pierced His hands, His feet, and His side. OBEDIENCE is not something she dreads, but an act of reciprocal sacrifice. He chose obedience to the cross for her; how can she possibly dread offering her will for Him? It is a small offering compared to His GREAT GIFT.

When her flesh is tempted to rise up and complain, or her heart entertains evil, she will remind herself how great His love is toward her. She will remind herself that He gave HIMSELF so that she might live. What is it to offer a small portion of her wayward flesh for so perfect a love?

So Samuel said: "Has the Lord as great delight in burnt offerings and sacrifices, As in obeying the voice of the Lord? Behold, to obey is better than sacrifice, And to heed than the fat of rams... (1 Samuel 15:22)

From His Heart to Mine . . .

Decision Time

Some bridges need to be burned. That relationship that drags you
down and makes you feel used. GOOD-BYE! That friend who
tempts you to sin and even brings it into your space. GOOD-BYE!
That offense you've nursed for years and continue to feed. GOOD-
BYE! That addiction you've thought held your very identity captive.
GOOD-BYE!

Today, the woman warrior for Christ is standing on the bridge
once more. On one side is green pastures, still waters, and a restored
soul. On the other side is dry grass, empty wells, and a withered heart.
Why is the decision even hard? She has gone back and forth across
the same bridge TOO MANY times.

No longer will she enable, condone or participate in sinful
behavior. She wants to honor her Lord—not bring shame to His
Name.

Today, she will burn that bridge, once and for all. God has
beautiful things waiting on the other side. Run to HIM!

*He restores my soul; He leads me in the paths of righteousness For His name's
sake. (Psalm 23:3)*

From His Heart to Mine . . .

Drink Him In

BITTER and SWEET have touched her lips. But from this day forth, the woman warrior for Christ will no longer sip from the enemy's cistern. He has paralyzed her long enough with his poison. His cup is filled with fear, shame, rejection, and hatred. Why would she want to drink filth when the Lord offers something far cleaner and sweeter?

Her heart is new and her mind washed clean. Her lips desire only goodness—drinking in the beauty, love, and holiness of a righteous and forgiving Lord. When He fills her, His mercy and grace overflow onto others.

Her heart's desire is to share Him with those she loves, but she knows she can only pour out what she has allowed poured in. She will guard her heart and her lips with all vigilance. She will drink in the Lord. He is her cup. He is her portion. He is her ALL in ALL.

Oh, taste and see that the Lord is good; Blessed is the man who trusts in Him! (Psalm 34:8)

From His Heart to Mine . . .

Hiding Place

Storms come. This is not heaven yet! SORROW beckons. ANGER tempts. LUST conspires. Every fleshly emotion claws her mind for attention, demanding to have its say. BUT GOD . . . speaks to the woman warrior in the midst of battle and tells her to hear ONLY HIM.

He reminds her to seek higher ground—a place of perseverance, peace, and rest. It is a safe place where the waters of life cannot pull her in and toss her about. There is protection in the cleft of the rock!

Assuredly, the storms will pass and the rainbow will come, but for now, HIDE IN HIM. Don't let the waves come near. Cling to the Lord—He is her Rock of Perseverance. Refuse to give up, refuse to give in, and refuse to retreat. TRUST HIM.

He who dwells in the secret place of the Most High Shall abide under the shadow of the Almighty. I will say of the LORD, "He is my refuge and my fortress; My God, in Him I will trust." (Psalm 91:1-2)

From His Heart to Mine . . .

Him Only

AT TIMES, He takes her breath away. His goodness, His mercy, His beauty, His magnificence, His holiness, His love. She sees others going about their busy lives and wonders . . . Do they even know HIM?

He makes this life meaningful! And yet, He gets pushed aside for the urgent, immediate, and even the mundane. There are times, EVERY DAY, when the woman warrior stops what she is doing, tells the chaos to wait, and sets her mind solely on HIM. He reminds her of what is truly important and what holds only temporary significance.

He keeps her spiritual house in order. He keeps her feet on the right path. And yes, He gives her the very breath He takes away. He is her LORD and NOTHING will surpass Him in her life. That is her desire! That is her DECLARATION!

For a day in Your courts is better than a thousand. I would rather be a doorkeeper in the house of my God Than dwell in the tents of wickedness (Psalm 84:10)

From His Heart to Mine . . .

DAY 40
Love Anyway

There is no greater wound than the wound that comes from "friendly" fire. The woman warrior knows those in the world will use her for target practice—shooting arrows into her life and attempting to assassinate her character with verbal barbs. She expects those attacks! But when it is someone close to her, the pain goes deep and renders her defenseless. It bypasses her armor and pierces her heart, taking her breath away and sending her to her knees.

It is not a wound she has the power to heal. ONLY GOD takes away such gripping pain. She MUST forgive; it is a commandment. Walking in offense is not an option. But ONLY GOD gives her the grace to do so.

ONLY GOD is the source of agape love. It is not in her flesh to offer, but IT IS IN JESUS, who lives on the inside of her. She must release the anguish, exchanging her hurt for a deeper love and more authentic walk. Pain "be gone." Let LOVE reign!

Then Jesus said, "Father, forgive them, for they do not know what they do."
(Luke 23:34)

From His Heart to Mine . . .

Cast Off Darkness

What to wear? What to wear? The woman warrior for Christ knows she has a choice, and chooses wisely.

When the enemy offers her a crown of condemnation . . . BY FAITH, she chooses to wear an imperishable crown of God's glory! When the enemy pushes moth-ridden garments at her and says, "Wear this!". . . BY FAITH, she chooses to wear a garment of praise! When the enemy insists she cover herself with ashes of mourning . . . BY FAITH, she chooses to wear the joy of HIS righteousness!

No more donning the enemy's garb! Old things are going out with the trash and never coming back into her house. From this day forth, she chooses to put on Christ Jesus. She will wear the ARMOR OF LIGHT.

The night is far spent, the day is at hand. Therefore let us cast off the works of darkness, and let us put on the armor of light. Let us walk properly, as in the day, not in revelry and drunkenness, not in lewdness and lust, not in strife and envy. But put on the Lord Jesus Christ, and make no provision for the flesh, to fulfill its lusts. (Romans 13:12-14)

From His Heart to Mine . . .

Eternal Treasure

The woman warrior knows what it is like to chase empty treasure. She has held fool's gold in her hand far too often! It only left her barren and cold. That changed the moment she met JESUS.

He became her eternal treasure. Now, her desire is to spend time with Him, getting to know Him better, and diving deeper into His character. She wants to lose herself in HIM—in His love, His kindness, and His mercy.

She wants to be like David—a man after God's own heart. Like Abraham—a friend of God. And like John—the disciple who placed his head upon Jesus' chest and heard the heartbeat of God.

Yes, her days of chasing temporal treasures are gone. Now, she runs after Jesus and the eternal. He is her GREATEST PURSUIT!

As the deer pants for the water brooks, So pants my soul for You, O God.
(Psalm 42:1)

From His Heart to Mine . . .

DAY 43
Thirsty for More

She gazes upon the empty well . . . THIRSTY. How did she find herself in such a dry place? Others seem to be full of the Spirit—joy shines within their eyes and grace flows from their lips. But she has nothing to offer. "Lord," she cries out. "I need a fresh touch!"

In His goodness, HE HEARS HER. He has waited beside the well, longing for her to call His Name—waiting for her to speak forth her need! The woman warrior is not her own source. Without the Lord, she will always thirst for more. He is her air, He is her sustenance, He is her LIVING WATER.

Just as He was with Moses and the Hebrew children in the desert, and just as He was with the woman of Samaria at the well, so He is with her. When dry times come, she remembers WHO is her source, and the well is empty no more.

Jesus answered and said to her, "Whoever drinks of this water will thirst again, but whoever drinks of the water that I shall give him will never thirst. But the water that I shall give him will become in him a fountain of water springing up into everlasting life." (John 4:13-14)

From His Heart to Mine . . .

She is Priceless

The woman warrior for Christ knows her value. Make no mistake—she is not arrogant. She does not walk in self-confidence, but in complete confidence in God.

She knows that no person, group or adversary determines her value. God never polled the masses before assigning her worth. He never thumbed through the pages of a magazine or looked at the big screen before deciding if she measured up. He never asked her family, her friends, or her mate for their input. He never even asked her!

He DEMONSTRATED her worth to Him when He left His heavenly home, laid His life upon the cross, and spoke, "It is finished." Her Lord paid too high of a price for her to let anyone or anything whisper "worthless" in her ear.

She will listen to ONE voice. She is HIS DAUGHTER. She is HIS SERVANT. She is HIS SOLDIER. Let her walk, rest, and abide in HIM.

For God so loved the world that He gave His only begotten Son, that whoever believes in Him should not perish but have everlasting life. John 3:16

From His Heart to Mine . . .

Tranquil Waters

He walks with her. He calls her by name. He whispers, "You are mine." The woman warrior for Christ knows she is NEVER alone. She hears her Lord's voice in the deepest night and the brightest day.

It's true that there are times when He feels far away, but she trusts the WORD of the LORD over what she feels. When she hits pause, and the world stops, she can sense His presence, even as the battle rages around her.

As she thinks on His Name, tranquil waters surround her and hope consumes her. The enemy can't have her. There is place for only ONE in her heart, and that belongs to Jesus. "Father, God, let us see and sense your presence today."

And they said to one another, "Did not our heart burn within us while He talked with us on the road, and while He opened the Scriptures to us?" (Luke 24:32)

From His Heart to Mine . . .

DAY 46

Trusting In Battle

Trust is one of the woman warrior's most PRIZED WEAPONS. She draws it from its sheath to protect her heart when skies are the darkest and hope is hardest to find. She carries it at her side as a reminder of God's sovereignty when blessings abound, and pride tempts her to take a bow. She holds it tightly in her grasp to keep herself steady when the ground beneath her feet shakes with unforeseen heartache and tears blur her vision.

Trust is the ONE WEAPON that makes sense when life makes no sense at all. Trust confounds the enemy's camp and supernaturally strengthens her spirit man. She WILL trust in the LORD—the Almighty—who is and who was and who is to come!

Praise His Holy Name! "Today, Lord, we trust in YOU!"

And He has on His robe and on His thigh a name written: KING OF KINGS AND LORD OF LORDS. (Revelations 19:16)

From His Heart to Mine . . .

Armed & Dangerous

Satan is never impressed with a show. There are times the woman warrior for Christ must remind herself . . . it is the Lord's strength that causes the enemy to flee—not her own.

She can stomp her feet, scream at demons, and make heavenly declarations all day long, but if she walks in defiance to the Commander . . . choosing the dictates of her flesh over a surrendered will . . . why is she surprised at the lethargic results she sees? VICTORY over the enemy comes when she SUBMITS herself to God—not the other way around!

She is "armed and dangerous" but only when she is armed with the Word of GOD and walking in the power of HIS MIGHT. He makes her dangerous to the kingdom of darkness. He causes the enemy to flee! To Him be the glory!

Therefore submit to God. Resist the devil and he will flee from you. Draw near to God and He will draw near to you. Cleanse your hands, you sinners; and purify your hearts, you double-minded. Lament and mourn and weep! Let your laughter be turned to mourning and your joy to gloom. Humble yourselves in the sight of the Lord, and He will lift you up. (James 4:7-10)

From His Heart to Mine . . .

DAY 48
Anticipation

The woman warrior senses CHANGE. It is not something she can name or even something she can confess. It is elusive, yet it is there, waiting to be born—much like a seed buried in the ground and about to burst from the darkness into the fullness of light.

Unspoken EXCITEMENT stirs within her heart as she waits to see what the Lord has in store! He is doing something He has not done before—something that only a Sovereign King has the power to make manifest. She will not try to guess, coerce, or even manipulate God's hand. She will wait in expectation.

She knows her Father loves to surprise His children. This is one of those times. "Yes, Lord, let it be so . . . quickly!"

Behold, I will do a new thing, Now it shall spring forth;
Shall you not know it? I will even make a road in the wilderness
And rivers in the desert. (Isaiah 43:19)

From His Heart to Mine . . .

DAY 49
He is Able

The woman warrior knows she cannot interfere in another's will, even if it is for their greater good. If only people were puppets and she could force them to accept God's plan for their life. But that is not how God orchestrated the world. He gave each person a will.

Changing someone DETERMINED to reject God's plan for his or her life is like trying to turn around a runaway ship with a lasso.

So what is she to do? SURRENDER. Stop fighting for control of the ship's wheel and trust that the true Navigator is more than able to take over. STEP BACK. Not in defeat … but so the Holy Spirit can step in. PRAY. For the power and might of Jesus Christ to manifest in the lives of those she loves. Pray that situations and circumstances are arranged and rearranged so they have every opportunity to FREELY turn toward Him. And, pray for the grace to keep her "hands off" while the ship is put back on course.

JESUS is able!

For His anger is but for a moment, His favor is for life: Weeping may endure for a night, But joy comes in the morning. (Psalm 30:5)

From His Heart to Mine . . .

DAY 50
The Grace Way

There are those who find pleasure thumbing through the tattered and torn pages of her past, reminiscing over the ugly parts of her life and reminding her of who she used to be. She has gone down memory lane with "those voices" for the last time.

NOW, the woman warrior is on a new journey—a journey of GRACE. While others may want her to feel less, GRACE tells her she is MORE—more beautiful, more beloved, and more precious than gold or silver. She will never again be a child of shame and sin.

She belongs to the KING; she is a child of GRACE. Man cannot take away what God has bestowed. Thank you, Jesus!

You are fairer than the sons of men; Grace is poured upon Your lips; Therefore God has blessed you forever. (Psalm 45:2)

From His Heart to Mine . . .

Attitude of Excellence

Positioned for PROMOTION. The woman warrior guards her attitude, especially in the heat of battle. Is she trusting God, knowing His character is good EVEN WHEN the situation is not? Or, is she moaning and groaning, demanding God make her happy "or else"?

Joseph had every reason to have a rotten attitude. Sold into slavery by his brothers, tossed into prison for a crime he never committed, and then forgotten by his cellmate for two long years. Why not grow bitter and angry?

But Joseph refused, and the Word says that God was with him. When the time was right, God promoted him to second in command beneath Pharaoh over ALL of Egypt. Joseph had authority over the very prison that once held him captive. He had authority over the very one who falsely accused him of a crime. And, he had authority over his brothers who sold him into slavery.

Promotion is coming, BUT FIRST the test. Put on your armor. Check your attitude. Get ready to live a life of excellence!

The refining pot is for silver and the furnace for gold, But the Lord tests the hearts. (Proverbs 17:3)

From His Heart to Mine . . .

The Intercessor's Heart

She still remembers the day she drew the line in the sand. Her heart bowed before the Lord and she declared that she would NEVER return to the enemy's camp. The woman warrior's allegiance is to JESUS and Him ONLY.

When she looks back, she has zero regrets. It has been a beautiful journey. BUT NOW ... she is seeing others she loves jump back and forth between dark and light, fraternizing with the enemy and then petitioning God, as if His grace is cheap and sin without consequence. How her heart breaks!

She will not let those she cares for be lured away without a fight. She will intercede in a spirit of compassion and faith—declaring the Word of God and trusting that He is able.

What He did in her life, He can do in theirs! Father, God. Have mercy. Forgive them. DRAW THEM to you by your mighty hand. In Jesus' Name. Amen.

... The effective, fervent prayer of a righteous man avails much. (James 5:16)

From His Heart to Mine . . .

Releasing the Pain

Well, that didn't go according to plan.

She thought she had made peace with her past. She checked it off her "to do" list with a wide, confident stroke of her spiritual pen. But that was before . . . before she came face to face with all that "should have" and "should not have" been.

Now, she is left holding the remnants of a shattered heart. If only tears and rage were enough to wash her clean—she would be healed and whole by now. But it doesn't work; it never has.

So, she does what any woman warrior for Christ should do. She picks up the broken pieces, takes them back to the altar, and surrenders the pain once again. Every time she makes the trip, the release lasts longer.

One day, she knows, she will leave the pain of her past on the altar and never see it again. Until then, she will trust JESUS in the process. He is her BURDEN BEARER.

Therefore humble yourselves under the mighty hand of God, that He may exalt you in due time, casting all your care upon Him, for He cares for you. (1 Peter 5:6-7)

From His Heart to Mine . . .

Life in Balance

The woman warrior knows she cannot allow the demands of others to override the voice of God. People will want to hand her projects and problems—obligating her to move, do, and help as THEY see fit. They will keep her hands and head so full of their "stuff" that she misses the opportunity to obey God.

Yes, she wants to be compassionate. Yes, she wants to show the love of Christ. Yes, she wants to put herself aside for others. But she must stop and ask: "Father, at what point am I helping and at what point am I hindering?"

Starting today, she will pause and reflect before answering a need. She will let God's Spirit direct her words and deeds. She will not be shaped or moved by the tug of her emotions, religious performance or desire for acceptance. Through it all, she WILL give them JESUS—He is MORE than enough.

Then Peter said, "Silver and gold I do not have, but what I do have I give you: In the name of Jesus Christ of Nazareth, rise up and walk." And he took him by the right hand and lifted him up, and immediately his feet and ankle bones received strength. (Acts 3:6-7)

From His Heart to Mine . . .

Be Still

The woman warrior has FAITH to face the storms. Though they may catch her by surprise at times, and may even sweep her off her feet, she is quick to regain her spiritual footing.

Her sails are sure and her anchor holds. She will not allow the enemy to toss her or her loved ones overboard! Winds of conflict may roar about her ears, and uncertainty slap against her like relentless waves, but she remains STEADFAST in her faith.

She has pushed back against fear. Prayer and praise have remained upon her lips. NOW, the time has come to put an end to it. NOW, the time has come to DECLARE the Word of the LORD over the storm. "PEACE, BE STILL."

And a great windstorm arose, and the waves beat into the boat, so that it was already filling. But He was in the stern, asleep on a pillow. And they awoke Him and said to Him, "Teacher, do You not care that we are perishing?" Then He arose and rebuked the wind, and said to the sea, "Peace, be still!" And the wind ceased and there was a great calm. (Mark 4:37-39)

From His Heart to Mine . . .

Prepare for Battle

The enemy does not stand down just because the woman warrior is on assignment from God!

Did Goliath cower in his tent when he saw David? Did the viper hide in the pile of wood when he spied Paul? Did Jezebel apologize to Elijah after fire came down from heaven? Expect obstacles. Expect adversity. But also EXPECT victory.

Let God show up and show out. Remember, it is HIS GLORY. Through HIM David defeated Goliath! Paul shook off the viper! Dogs devoured Jezebel! Many times, the greater the battle, the greater God's demonstration of power.

Trust Him in the fray, and know that there would be no need for a warrior's heart if there were no battles. Stay strong in the faith, pray for discernment, and walk in obedience. The LORD God is able!

He [Abraham] did not waver at the promise of God through unbelief, but was strengthened in faith, giving glory to God, and being fully convinced that what He had promised He was also able to perform. (Romans 4:20-21)

From His Heart to Mine . . .

DAY 57
In His Time

Progress is not always pretty, but it is BEAUTIFUL. The woman warrior knows that higher spiritual ground is captured through battle—she has the cuts, bumps, and bruises to prove it!

When her mind and mouth trip her up, she simply stops, regroups, repents, and goes at it again. She KNOWS she is not perfect, but refuses to cling to self-remorse or wave the white flag before a defeated enemy. Time is too precious to linger in that wasteland!

She will submit her defeats AND her victories to her Lord. He alone will make all things BEAUTIFUL, in HIS time.

But we all, with unveiled face, beholding as in a mirror the glory of the Lord, are being transformed into the same image from glory to glory, just as by the Spirit of the Lord. (2 Corinthians 3:18)

From His Heart to Mine . . .

You Are Chosen

CHOSEN. Let the word sink deep within your spirit. Performance demands perfection before acceptance—laughing at your flawed efforts and mocking your failures.

It says: "You are not good enough." "Your faith is too weak today." And, "You want God to love you? Then, try harder!"

But the WORD of the LORD says, "My yoke is easy." The WORD of the LORD says, "It is by grace you are saved through faith—not by works." The WORD of the LORD says, "You are accepted in the Beloved."

While salvation compels you to love, serve, and minister, approval is found ONLY in HIM. You do not have to meet the constantly evolving standards set by others. It is too late to buy into that lie. The woman warrior knows . . . SHE IS CHOSEN.

He found him in a desert land
And in the wasteland, a howling wilderness;
He encircled him, He instructed him,
He kept him as the apple of His eye.
(Deuteronomy 32:10)

From His Heart to Mine . . .

Awaken Sister Soldiers

God's hand has always been upon her. She sees that now. From an early age, the enemy chipped away at her—the cruel names, stinging rejection, pain of abandonment, and the anguish of being used. It seemed as if the enemy sensed the slumbering warrior spirit inside her and sought to destroy her early.

But in GOD'S TIMING . . .

He roused the sleeping soldier and called her forth for His army. He said, "You are EXACTLY who I want with me." All her flaws, shame, sin and pain fell away under the banner of His righteous blood and unconditional love. And all the wounds wrought by the enemy? They had only made her stronger.

Today she proclaims: She won't give in. She won't give up. She won't give ground. She is a woman warrior FOR Christ. Hallelujah!

And we know that all things work together for good to those who love God, to those who are the called according to His purpose. (Romans 8:28)

From His Heart to Mine . . .

DAY 60
Unmerited Favor

FAVOR of the KING. She needs it NOW—SUPERNATURAL preference that compels goodness and mercy to surround her.

Favor opens doors of opportunity, causes light to shine upon her face, and even makes enemies give gifts to her. The woman warrior knows it is a portion of her INHERITANCE! It is the beauty of being a child of the King.

She will not take favor for granted or treat it with disdain. She will BELIEVE in, SPEAK forth, and TRUST in GOD'S UNMERITED FAVOR. It is so very good to walk in the King's court. It is so good to have His face shine upon hers.

For You, O LORD, will bless the righteous; With favor You will surround him as with a shield. (Psalm 5:12)

From His Heart to Mine . . .

Never Alone

God has not abandoned her on the battlefield! He is with her—her Shield and Strong Tower!

The woman warrior stands firm on the truth that JESUS sits on the throne. She does not serve a defeated foe, but the KING of kings and LORD of lords. The FIRST and the LAST, and the great I AM.

She may have to walk through the valley, but she is NEVER alone or unarmed. The SWORD OF THE SPIRIT is in her mouth. When she speaks the Word in faith, the enemy hears the voice of God Almighty and scatters.

Fear belongs to Satan's army. It has no place in the Lord's camp.

You believe there is one God. You do well. Even the demons believe—and tremble (James 2:19)

From His Heart to Mine . . .

A Daniel Attitude

It is no surprise that she finds herself in this situation. God's greatest glory is often revealed in the fiery furnace or in the lion's den.

She could have chosen to compromise. She could have chosen to remain silent. Or, she could have chosen to use such diplomatic, sugary words that no one really knew her stance. BUT GOD . . .

This was not a time to take the easy way out. It was not the time to bow her flesh to people-pleasing pressure. Yes, she knows that love must prevail; her heart knows that as well. But her spirit will not lie for another's comfort. She will not condemn—she will speak TRUTH in LOVE.

She is a child of God, not a child of the world. The LORD has her allegiance. He will not forsake her. Selah.

Now when Daniel knew that the writing was signed, he went home. And in his upper room, with his windows open toward Jerusalem, he knelt down on his knees three times that day, and prayed and gave thanks before his God, as was his custom since early days. (Daniel 6:10)

From His Heart to Mine . . .

Still Small Voice

She wants to hear HIS voice—the voice of her Maker. The enemy brings noise clutter—spamming her mind with doubts and confusion. Just as Satan pursued Eve in the garden, so he tempts the woman warrior to question God's perfect plan.

BUT THE LORD SAYS: "Pursue Me. You will know My will." When she stops chasing the noise, and starts chasing God with a relentless, passionate heart, she will find His will.

He is not in the chaos. He is not in the confusion. He is in the PEACE.

… And behold, the Lord passed by, and a great and strong wind tore into the mountains and broke the rocks in pieces before the Lord, but the Lord was not in the wind; and after the wind an earthquake, but the Lord was not in the earthquake; and after the earthquake a fire, but the Lord was not in the fire; and after the fire a still small voice. (1 Kings 19:11-12)

From His Heart to Mine . . .

Resurrection Power

ONLY GOD can turn a dead end into a detour. The woman warrior is not giving up on those she loves! The enemy tells her it is hopeless; he aims the arrow of despair at her heart. Well-meaning friends tell her to wash her hands; they counsel her against wasting her time and casting her pearls before swine.

If not for her faith, it would be easy to give in. But the woman warrior reminds herself that the Lord did not give up on her, and she is not giving up on others.

While her flesh may want to surrender, her spirit reminds her that she serves a powerful Lord. He has given her weapons to fight back! She deflects the fiery darts of the enemy and the negative words of others with her shield of faith, pushing him back with the promises of God.

Her Lord is the resurrection AND the life—in every situation and circumstance. She knows HOPE is ALIVE in Him! Amen.

And he who had died came out bound hand and foot with graveclothes, and his face was wrapped with a cloth. Jesus said to them, "Loose him, and let him go." (John 11:44)

From His Heart to Mine . . .

Why Fear?

Fear is a harsh taskmaster, DEMANDING bricks without straw, taking more and leaving less. The woman warrior refuses to bow her knee to the Oppressor. Her days of living in chains are OVER. She holds fast to her Deliverer—the One who parted the Red Sea, crushed the enemy, and set the captives free.

There was a time when she allowed fear to dictate her days, keeping her from moving in the purpose and plans of the Almighty. Fear of failure, fear of success, fear of speaking, fear of walking in her calling, fear of loss, fear of lack, fear of . . .

Those days are gone. Fear has no right to touch her! She is REDEEMED! Now, she walks in the knowledge that if God calls her to it, He will walk with her through it. With the very Creator on her side, what is there to fear?

But now, thus says the Lord, who created you, O Jacob, And He who formed you, O Israel: "Fear not, for I have redeemed you; I have called you by your name; You are Mine. (Isaiah 43:1)

From His Heart to Mine . . .

DAY 66
Reaching Forward

She was ALL in. Like a freight train on a one-way track. But now
. . . broken and bruised, the woman warrior doesn't understand how
she got here.

The voices mock her, asking, "What were you thinking? Were you
really that blind to the warning signs, or did you choose not to see?"
She will not wallow in the mire with the naysayers in her life. She has
too much to do!

The woman warrior refuses to linger at the wreckage of her error
or wrongly placed trust. Others may want to stay behind and gawk,
but they will not find her there. She is going on with GOD and the
GOOD PLAN He has for her life. AMEN!

Brethren, I do not count myself to have apprehended; but one thing I do, forgetting
those things which are behind and reaching forward to those things which are
ahead... (Philippians 3:13)

From His Heart to Mine . . .

Pushing Through

Her FAITH cries: "If she can but TOUCH the hem of HIS garment ..." The woman warrior will not be held back! She has settled for "lack and less" long enough.

She may have to push through the crowd of her emotions—insecurity, fear, shyness, shame, regret, and sorrow—but she will not let her feelings dictate her healing. She has waited too long for this moment. She is ready to be set free from spiritual, mental, and physical limitations.

She draws CLOSER to Him, for in His presence, in His touch, and in His glance, there is wholeness, truth and peace. In Him there is POWER. She will not quit until she touches HIM.

And Jesus, immediately knowing in Himself that power had gone out of Him, turned around in the crowd and said, "Who touched my clothes?" (Mark 5:30)

From His Heart to Mine . . .

All She Needs

PANIC is not a word in her vocabulary. While others may fret and fear, she holds fast to the knowledge of Who is her FATHER.

The very One who knit her in her mother's womb is more than able to handle any situation life throws her direction. She simply must remember to hold her poise and trust that God is with her.

She is not surprised by the enemy's wiles. She already knows he will try to snare her attention and distract her with fearful thoughts, but she trusts that the Holy Spirit surrounds her with His presence.

When she turns to the right, He is there. When she turns to the left, He is there. He is her constant covering. He is HER peace-giver, HER protector, and HER provider. He is all she needs.

But my God shall supply all your need according to his riches in glory by Christ Jesus. (Philippians 4:19)

From His Heart to Mine . . .

He Always Hears

Blind-sided! She did not see THAT ONE coming! The pain . . .
the tears . . . the brokenness. Even still, the woman warrior will not
lay down. Why would she want to give glory to the devil?

While the sorrow is raw and the emotions are real, so is the God
she trusts—He never sleeps nor slumbers. His Holy Spirit lives within
her and reminds her that she is loved. She does not have to walk
through any trial alone!

She will CALL UPON the Name of JESUS. He IS the burden
bearer. He wipes away her tears. He renews her hope. YES . . . He
alone is her ALL in ALL.

*But You, O LORD, are a shield for me, My glory and the One who lifts my
head. I cried to the LORD with my voice, And He heard me from His holy hill.
Selah. (Psalm 3:3-4)*

From His Heart to Mine . . .

DAY 70
Believe Him

Temptation and offense are mere distractions from a defeated foe—meant to lure the woman warrior away from her true purpose.

The evil one knows that God has a beautiful plan for her life, and wants nothing more than to see her fail. The woman warrior refuses to give ground! She will not let fear, doubt or unbelief take her down the wrong path. She purposely prays and seeks the Lord's face—trusting that He will hold her hand and direct her steps.

HIS WILL is her heart's desire, LOVE is her high calling and FAITH her banner. She will not let her faith grow weak or her love grow cold! She WILL keep believing. She WILL keep trusting. She WILL see the mountain move!

So Jesus said to them, "… for assuredly, I say to you, if you have faith as a mustard seed, you will say to this mountain, 'Move from here to there,' and it will move; and nothing will be impossible for you." (Matthew 17:20)

From His Heart to Mine . . .

DAY 71
At His Feet

ENJOY HIS PRESENCE! Why do we let ourselves fall into the performance trap? Do we really think God's approval is fickle—won or lost on any given day, depending on our behavior or His mood? Are we so powerful that we can make the blood of Jesus of no effect because we have yet to be perfected?

When will we understand that our atonement is based on the work of the cross and our KNOWING Jesus. Yes, the woman warrior knows that faith without works is dead, but so is faith without relationship. Then, it's simply faith in works and profits her nothing.

Instead of seeking opportunities to impress God or gain the affirmation of people, the woman warrior turns her heart toward LOVING the Lord and SEEKING His face. How beautiful it is to simply enjoy a relationship with the One she loves.

Now it happened as they went that He entered a certain village; and a certain woman named Martha welcomed Him into her house. And she had a sister called Mary, who also sat at Jesus' feet and heard His word. (Luke 10:38-39)

From His Heart to Mine . . .

His Beloved

A woman warrior is not defined by her shape, size or shade. The enemy will say she is "not enough" – even criticize and compare her to others who are "more than." But her Lord says: YOU ARE MY BELOVED.

The very One who created her longs to spend quiet time with her. She is not a bother to Him! He seeks to know her better; to touch her heart with His mercy and His grace. He has secrets He wants to share with only her; words that are meant for her ears alone. He does not treat their relationship with carelessness, but with an unconditional love that surrounds her heart and stills her soul. He sees the inward person, and He says . . .

You are wonderfully made. Rest in my arms. Let me love you— without barriers or boundaries. LET ME love you—right where you are. You are accepted. You are MINE.

...to the praise of the glory of His grace, by which He made us accepted in the Beloved. (Ephesians 1:6)

From His Heart to Mine . . .

DAY 73

Seek Peace

The woman warrior knows to pursue PEACE. When confusion entangles her mind and life's demands become crashing waves, she calls upon the ONE who commands the sea, the stars, and even the grave.

While it is true that life is not always quiet and the world does not always stop for her needs, she has the full assurance that when she prays to her Lord, HE HEARS. He is not a God she is unable to touch. He is not a deity with little concern for His creation. He is a loving Lord who sacrificed Himself that she might be saved.

JESUS.

Just His Name calms her soul and soothes her spirit. He IS her PEACE.

For unto us a Child is born, Unto us a Son is given; And the government will be upon His shoulder. And His name will be called Wonderful, Counselor, Mighty God, Everlasting Father, Prince of Peace. (Isaiah 9:6)

From His Heart to Mine . . .

The Victor's Crown

The woman warrior refuses to wear the victim's crown. She belongs to the King of Glory! Self-pity is not her heritage.

When she is tempted to feel sorry for herself or say, "Why me, Lord?" she reminds herself of the great sacrifice Jesus made on her behalf. Does it really honor her Lord to complain about her life?

Yes, she has known hardship, but so have many others. She is not alone. Now, she must decide if she wants to walk around in the chains of self-pity or walk away from what has held her bound.

God has good plans for her life! But she must FIRST leave the victim's cabin before she can explore the King's castle.

Cast your cares on the LORD and he will sustain you; he will never let the righteous be shaken. (Psalm 55:22)

From His Heart to Mine . . .

DAY 75
The Throne Room

There is a SECRET PLACE where the woman warrior for Christ
draws strength; times of refreshing only come from His Presence.
When they are alone, His voice becomes clearer and His heart more
tangible.

Some call the place their war room. Others call it their prayer
closet. She has learned that the name is not nearly as important as
what happens when she gets alone with the Lord. Prayers of faith go
up before the THRONE of GOD like a sweet aroma.

She does not doubt that her Lord hears her petitions and her
praise. She knows her prayers avail much, for her faith is firmly
established on the Lord's righteousness. She walks in confidence,
BECAUSE she walks with Him.

*But you, when you pray, go into your room, and when you have shut your door,
pray to your Father who is in the secret place; and your Father who sees in secret
will reward you openly. (Matthew 6:6)*

From His Heart to Mine . . .

DAY 76

Trust and Release

Her knuckles are white from HOLDING ON. She needs relief. Her energy is spent, her prayers never cease, and yet . . . the burden is still there.

But the Lord would say, "WHY are you holding on? Let go!" He will not pry anything out of her hands. But when she releases what is so dear . . . when she releases what is beyond her control . . . when she releases what consumes her thoughts . . . THEN, the LORD can catch it within His mighty hands.

The woman warrior for Christ knows this truth. Now, she needs to put the knowledge into practice. Now, she must choose to walk in the trust she so easily professes. Now, she must choose to let go of what she holds tightly in her grasp. God has got this! "Father, God, give us the grace to TRUST and RELEASE!"

The Lord also will be a refuge for the oppressed, A refuge in times of trouble. And those who know Your name will put their trust in You; For You, Lord, have not forsaken those who seek You. (Psalm 9:9-10)

From His Heart to Mine . . .

DAY 77
God-Given Authority

The woman warrior for Christ does NOT stand passively on the sidelines of life, taking body blows from the enemy as if she is defenseless. She spent too many years of her life as Satan's punching bag. NO MORE!

Now, she KNOWS her identity is in Christ and her strength comes from Him alone. Now, she is the one on attack—PUSHING BACK the one who seeks only to steal, kill, and destroy. Her Lord is not helpless and hopeless, and neither is she!

The Commander of Angel Armies has placed holy weapons in her hands—giving her the discernment to see the enemy's ploys and the authority to destroy the works of darkness. Now is not the time to doubt her position in Christ. Now is the time to ACT on behalf of those she loves. Now is the time to walk in her God-ordained authority! JESUS reigns!

Behold, I give you the authority to trample on serpents and scorpions, and over all the power of the enemy, and nothing shall by any means hurt you. (Luke 10:19)

From His Heart to Mine . . .

All In

The woman warrior walks in the INTEGRITY of her heart. She does not chase after sin, but resists it at every turn. Yes, she knows she is saved by grace, but she also knows that grace came at a sacrificial price for her Lord, and does not regard it lightly.

When she stumbles, she gets back up, and continues moving forward. There will ALWAYS be those who say, "Stay down! That's where you belong!" She recognizes the voice of the enemy and will not listen.

God has her WHOLE heart, but He also has her hand. He will lift her up. He will give her grace. And, He will bestow His mercy upon her— once again. He is the King of kings and Lord of lords, but she never forgets that He is also the One she calls, "Abba, Father . . ."

For as many as are led by the Spirit of God, these are sons of God. For you did not receive the spirit of bondage again to fear, but you received the Spirit of adoption by whom we cry out, "Abba, Father." (Romans 8:14-15)

From His Heart to Mine . . .

Speak Blessings

The woman warrior for Christ brings LIGHT and LIFE wherever she steps her foot. She will not speak evil over her life or the lives of others. Darkness and death were never meant to reside upon her tongue. God has a better plan!

Starting TODAY, she will use her words to speak forth BLESSING, not cursing. She will sow a harvest of encouragement and edification into the lives of others, knowing that in time, she will reap what she sows.

And . . . while she still has wounds from hurtful words spoken over her life, she will TRUST God's healing hand AND the power of His Word! For every negative thought that tries to ambush her, she will overcome with the TRUTH: "I am blessed, I am redeemed, I am one with Christ. No weapon formed against me will prosper!"

Hallelujah! Thank you, Jesus!

Let the words of my mouth and the meditation of my heart
Be acceptable in Your sight,
O Lord, my strength and my Redeemer.
(Psalm 19:14)

From His Heart to Mine . . .

Changing Seasons

The woman warrior is not a fair-weather Christian. Winter, spring, summer, fall—she knows ALL the seasons and would not bypass a single one.

Through the cold and dead days of winter, she learns to persevere by the power of the Holy Spirit. Through the showers of blessings and new beginnings of spring, she celebrates with the joy of the Lord. Through the spiritually dry and thirsty days of summer, she clings to the Rock all the more. Through the quiet and peaceful times of fall, she rests in the Savior's arms, renewing her strength for the days ahead.

She has learned that in EVERY SEASON there is beauty. Not one moment is wasted in God's timetable. Though doubt and confusion tempt her to look their way, she knows she is where she is supposed to be at this moment in time. She never drops her weapons and she never deserts her post—winter, spring, summer, fall—she is in the Lord's army for ALL her days.

To everything there is a season,
A time for every purpose under heaven
(Ecclesiastes 3:1)

From His Heart to Mine . . .

Run to Him

In the heat of the battle . . . the woman warrior for Christ RUNS to HIM! There was a time when she thought others could save her, when addiction sought to steal her, and when her heart tried to deceive her. Those days are gone!

While the enemy wants her paralyzed by doubt and fear, she refuses to be a prisoner of his plans! Rocky marriage? Rebellious children? Hard workplace? Failing health? Insufficient finances? She knows there is but ONE place to seek shelter. Nothing is too hard for her Lord. HER FAITH rests in HIM.

Nothing, and no one else, can work all things together for her good. Yes, she will choose to RUN to HIM.

The name of the Lord is a strong tower; The righteous run to it and are safe. (Proverbs 18:10)

From His Heart to Mine . . .

Peace in Waiting

SHE WILL WAIT. God will speak; His timing is perfect. For now, she stands still with her spiritual ears and eyes wide open.

She expects Him to respond, but knows she cannot force His hand. When worried faces want to know, "What are you going to do?!" The woman warrior speaks with certainty, "I am going to wait on the Lord."

He alone has the WISDOM to create the universe. He alone has the POWER to conquer the grave. He alone has the PEACE that passes all understanding. Is this too hard for Him?

When carnal reasoning tugs on her mind like a constant drone, and the enemy urges her to chase after fear, she will stand her ground with quiet confidence. She knows from where her help comes. Why would she worry? He WILL answer.

Show me Your ways, O Lord;
Teach me Your paths.
Lead me in Your truth and teach me,
For You are the God of my salvation;
On You I wait all the day.
(Psalm 25:4-5)

From His Heart to Mine . . .

Holding On

To know Jesus is to know joy unspeakable, love unconditional, and suffering that only comes from a fallen world. The woman warrior does not pretend life has no heartaches—she has faced plenty. What she knows is that her GOD is greater than this life.

Her God is the resurrected One—the One who conquered the grave and sits at the right hand of the Father. Because JESUS lives, she speaks hope over situations that bring heartache and rejects the voices that say it is impossible. The God who made man out of dust and breathed life into his lungs is more than able!

She will pray for spiritual eyesight, to see what the Lord would have her see, and not what the world offers. His goodness surrounds her and His grace holds her. The hardship is almost over. Blessings are coming! She speaks it and she believes it!

And Elisha prayed, and said, "Lord, I pray, open his eyes that he may see." Then the Lord opened the eyes of the young man, and he saw. And behold, the mountain was full of horses and chariots of fire all around Elisha. (2 Kings 6:17)

From His Heart to Mine . . .

The Lord's Victory

Did she forget to thank Him? In her excitement of answered prayer and hope restored, did she forget to appreciate the fact that her Lord is a TURNAROUND God?

Just when the woman warrior is weary from lifting her shield, and her shoulders ache from thrusting her sword, the Commander steps in and turns the battle in her favor. She had just about waved the white flag. She had just about made the enemy's day.

BUT GOD SAID, "Not going to happen." Today will not be a day for the enemy to celebrate. There is victory in the Lord's Camp! The woman warrior will praise His Name for He has done GREAT and MIGHTY things. "Yes, Lord, THANK YOU for the answered prayer—the glory is yours and yours alone!" Praise the Name of JESUS!

And one of them [lepers], when he saw that he was healed, returned, and with a loud voice glorified God, and fell down on his face at His feet, giving Him thanks ... So Jesus answered and said, "Were there not ten cleansed? But where are the nine? Were there not any found who returned to give glory to God except this foreigner?" (Luke 17:15-18)

From His Heart to Mine . . .

Sweet Strength

Once again, she has allowed distractions to drown out the voice of the Holy Spirit. She hurries about her day, tossing prayers into heaven like crumbs at squawking seagulls, hoping some of them are caught. Then, she runs to the next place, project or person with little thought of the majesty of God or the direction He would have her go.

In her careless, preoccupied mind, her sword becomes dull and her inner soldier grows weak. The battles come quick and hard, for the enemy senses her spiritual state. But God, in His mercy, will not leave her to be devoured!

She is HIS DAUGHTER. He fills her with living water and anoints her head with oil. His love is consuming. It draws her close to Him. In moments of intimate fellowship, He sharpens her sword and restores her hope. There is no sweeter time than in His courts. She will slow down and listen to what the Lord desires to say. There is strength in His presence.

We love Him because He first loved us. (1 John 4:19)

From His Heart to Mine . . .

Mountain Dweller

How she loves to linger on the mountaintop! The woman warrior for Christ cherishes such moments, for she knows too well what it is like to walk through the valley. It is in her KNOWING that she extends compassion to those who are struggling—those who are facing their own battles.

She will not treat them with prideful disdain—the attitude that says, "Thank you, Lord, that I'm not like sister so-and-so." Nor will she entertain the accuser of the brethren, "You know she's a sinner! She is getting what she deserves." THAT attitude is a quick ticket back to her own, well-worn valley!

Instead, the woman warrior will PUSH PRIDE aside and lift others before the throne of God with ALL humility. That is the heart and the attitude of a mountain-dweller. That is the heart and attitude of a Sister Soldier in Christ!

He has shown you, O man, what is good; And what does the Lord require of you But to do justly, To love mercy, And to walk humbly with your God? (Micah 6:8)

From His Heart to Mine . . .

The Answer

The woman warrior for Christ releases all she is, or will ever be, to the God of the past, present and future. The GREAT I AM knows the path He has for her. Does she really have the right to question Him? Does the clay have the right to question the potter? Does the canvas have the right to question the artist?

He has shown His love through the fire and through the ashes. He has shown His love through the joy and through the laughter. Through every moment of her life, He has been with her. Why would He leave her now?

This is a time of decision, but when she releases the outcome . . . when she puts on the garment of praise . . . when she refuses to push or prod . . . when she simply rests in His love . . .

"Yes, Lord, you know the answer. You ARE the answer. I will trust in you."

Jesus said to them, "Most assuredly, I say to you, before Abraham was, I AM."
(John 8:58)

From His Heart to Mine . . .

Hope of the Redeemed

Condemnation knocks at the door. It begs, "Let me come in again. I'm comfortable in your house."

The woman warrior has had enough of his visits. He stays entirely too long and takes up entirely too much space. There is no time or room for him in her life now.

She will not focus on what has been. Her attention is on the HERE AND NOW, and the days TO COME. The clothes she used to wear—shame, criticism, disapproval—those are no longer her garments! Now, she wears a garment of praise. Her Lord has clothed her in white. He has made her a new creation!

Her face is set on the goodness of her Creator. Her attention is set on learning His word and meditating upon His truth. Her heart is set on praising His name and praying for others. Condemnation has no place in her life. She KNOWS she is redeemed.

Oh, give thanks to the Lord, for He is good! For His mercy endures forever. Let the redeemed of the Lord say so, Whom He has redeemed from the hand of the enemy... (Psalm 107:1-2)

From His Heart to Mine . . .

DAY 89

First Love

The woman warrior for Christ senses God calling her to a deeper place of intimacy. There is a restlessness in her spirit that she knows is God examining her heart.

Like a traveler who has unintentionally veered away from her destination, she checks the compass of her soul. The Holy Spirit whispers, "This way. Come to me." She turns from the distractions and allure of the world. Nothing satisfies a disquieted spirit like the Lord.

With her face looking toward a new direction, and her heart once again consumed with the love of Jesus, she will spend time with HIM. Yes, daily chores must be done and life has demands, but in HIM, everything has a place. There is balance when HE is her first pursuit.

Nevertheless I have this against you, that you have left your first love. (Revelation 2:4)

From His Heart to Mine . . .

DAY 90

Every Good Gift

This is not the first battle she has fought. She has scars and stories to share with her sisters. Each time the enemy attacked, the Lord stood beside her. He brought her through the pain, the chaos, and the grief—stronger than before and more prepared to meet the next challenge.

Not once did He leave her behind on the battlefield, wounded and bleeding, to be toyed with by a ruthless enemy! She called on JESUS, and He came!

Time and time again, He rescued her from the sword and the snare of the enemy. Her scars are only reminders of all she has overcome, by the power and might of Jesus Christ. He is a good God and His mercy endures forever—she knows in whom she believes!

Every good gift and every perfect gift is from above, and comes down from the Father of lights, with whom there is no variation or shadow of turning. Of His own will He brought us forth by the word of truth, that we might be a kind of firstfruits of His creatures. (James 1:17-18)

From His Heart to Mine . . .

Please take a few minutes . . .

If you enjoyed reading the *Woman Warrior for Christ 90-Day Devotional*, we invite you to take just a few minutes to leave your review on Amazon.com.

Your feedback will help ensure more women hear about us and have the opportunity to join the Sister Soldiers in Christ ranks.

Also, please consider subscribing to the Sister Soldiers in Christ blog: SisterSoldiersinChrist.com and joining our Facebook page.

Thank you and God bless!